ONE TRIBE
AT A TIME

The Paper that Changed
the War in Afghanistan

J I M   G A N T

US ARMY, RET.

Black Irish Entertainment LLC

NEW YORK   LOS ANGELES

INTRODUCTION

Among the earliest readers of *One Tribe at a Time* was Gen. David Petraeus. One of the most recent was Osama bin Laden.

Petraeus read *One Tribe* and told his staff, "Operationalize this."

Bin Laden read it and circled the author's name on the title page. In the margin he wrote, "Kill this man."

I first met Special Forces Major Jim Gant in the summer of 2009. At the time I had a small website called "It's the Tribes, Stupid." The primary content on the site was five short videos that I had made with the intention of influencing policy in the Pentagon and the White House. I was hoping to get the decision-makers' attention on the subject of how the US was employing its forces in Afghanistan.

The message was, well ... "It's the tribes, Stupid."

Of course no one listened. No one even knew the site existed.

Then I met Jim.

The tribal concepts that I was talking about in theory, Jim had enacted in fact. He and I spent three days together at his home near Fort Bragg. Jim told me about leading Special Forces team ODA 316 in the Konar Valley in Afghanistan in 2003. He and his men had lived with the Mohmand tribe, had been taken in as brothers by the tribe's leaders; Jim himself had virtually been adopted as a son by the tribal chief, Noor Afzhal.

Was the US military's current strategy in Afghanistan doomed to failure? Would a tribally-based strategy have a better chance? Did Jim have an idea what an effective T.E.

(Tribal Engagement) design would look like?

Yes, we concluded. And yes, and yes.

"Jim," I said, "you have to write it."

Jim of course had already worked it out in his head. The document would be a white paper, about fifty pages long.

"If you write it," I promised him, "I'll bring it out on the website."

You always hope that something will go viral. Your aim is for a paper to get picked up and passed around.

That's what happened with *One Tribe at a Time*. Gen. James Mattis responded first, giving the paper a boost within the Marine Corps. *Small Wars Journal* picked it up next and added to the momentum. Even its detractors helped. A few high-snark attacks added to the paper's visibility.

Then Gen. Petraeus gave it his blessing.

One Tribe at a Time changed policy.

It also destroyed Jim Gant's career.

Jim's story became the basis for the bestseller *American Spartan: The Promise, the Mission, and the Betrayal of Special Forces Major Jim Gant* by former *Washington Post* reporter Ann Scott Tyson.

Alas, *One Tribe* did not change policy enough. It was too radical. Too disruptive to the battlespace owners. Too impractical within the sphere of Afghan-US politics. Tribal engagement was an idea whose time had not come, at least when implemented by conventional Army forces. But this short paper became a significant footnote in what will probably be the United States' last intervention of choice in the heartland of any Islamic nation or predominantly tribal culture.

Two final notes and I'll let you get on to the meat of the book.

1. The reason I came to believe, in the first place, that an understanding of tribes and the tribal mindset was essential to formulating a military and political strategy in Afghanistan was Alexander the Great. I studied Alexander's history in the Afghan kingdoms in the 330s BCE. He and his army ran into the same buzz-saw that we Yanks blundered into. This was not hard to predict. A Western-style invasion force (whether Macedonian, Roman, Russian, or American) could expect fierce, unconventional resistance on the home turf of a primitive, tribe-based society.

But here's the interesting part: Alexander was pre-Christian and his enemies were pre-Islamic. What that said to me was that religion could be taken out of the equation in attempting to understand the fight on the ground in Afghanistan. We couldn't chalk up our troubles to Islamic extremism or Islamo-fascism or Islamo-anything, because Islam didn't exist in Alexander's day. It wouldn't appear for another 900 years.

Tribalism.

Tribalism was the common dynamic between the East-West clash then and the East-West struggle now.

2. In the winter of 2010, Jim Gant and I, along with an Afghan tribal chief, Ajmal Khan Zazai, and our friend Michael McClellan, laid a brief siege to Washington DC, attempting to influence policy. We spoke at Marine Corps University and at Annapolis, gave a few interviews, and pleaded our case at several influential think tanks.

At CNAS, the Center for a New American Security, Jim pitched his concept of Tribal Engagement to the full team of scholars including the distinguished author and foreign affairs expert Robert Kaplan and CEO and former Afghan-vet Recon Marine captain Nate Fick. It was clear to all in attendance that Major Gant could, if given the chance, pull off the Lawrence-of-Arabia-type stunt of embedding with an Afghan tribe and making a tribal engagement scenario work. But who else could do it? Did the army have a secret reserve of officers who could pull off this kind of miracle? Did the Marine Corps?

Andrew Exum is a former Army Ranger captain with Afghan combat service (and author of *This Man's Army,* as well as the much-followed counterinsurgency blog *Abu Muqawama*.) He is also a Fellow at CNAS.

"Jim," Andrew said that afternoon, "after listening to you speak and looking in your eyes, I have no doubt that you could insert yourself into a tribal environment in Afghanistan and make this kind of program work. But I don't see how the United States can be realistically expected to back a policy that can only be implemented by geniuses."

Andrew was right. He had Jim pegged.

Gen. Petraeus was right too. So was Osama bin Laden.

Herewith: *One Tribe at a Time*.

See if you agree.

Steven Pressfield
March 2014

PREFACE

"I emphasized at the beginning of this paper that I am neither a strategist nor an academic. I know there will be many criticisms that span all levels of war, from military personnel to pundits. But I also know this: I will get on a helicopter tonight, armed with an AK-47 and three hundred rounds of ammunition and put my life on the line and my strategy to the test. Will you do the same?"

— *One Tribe at a Time*
Major Jim Gant,
US Army Special Forces
October 2009

The publication of *One Tribe at a Time* in October 2009 changed the course of my life and the lives of many others forever. In June 2010, I deployed to Afghanistan for nearly two years, and, together with some great men, put into action the ideas in *One Tribe at a Time.*

It worked.

I learned a great deal—including how much I still don't know. But I would without hesitation get on that same helicopter for Konar this very night, and do it again.

Captain Jim Gant (US Army, Ret.)
March 2014

ONE TRIBE AT A TIME

TABLE OF CONTENTS

A NOTE TO
THE READER

The thoughts and ideas that I will put forward in this paper are mine alone. Although I credit the US Army Special Forces for the training I have received and the trust of its commanders, nothing in this paper reflects the ideas and thinking of any other person or organization.

I am not a professional writer. I am not implying by writing this paper that anyone has "got it wrong" or that I have all the right answers. I don't.

I started writing this paper in January of '09 prior to the "New Afghanistan Plan." Much has changed since then. It is an extremely difficult and elusive situation in Afghanistan.

This paper is about tactical employment of small, well-trained units that, when combined with a larger effort, will have positive strategic implications.

The following is a short list of terms you will see in this paper. I will define others as they appear:

TET stands for "Tribal Engagement Teams." I will go into detail about them in Chapter 8, but they are referred to in many places prior to that.

TTE refers to "Tactical Tribal Engagement."

TES refers to "Tribal Engagement Strategy."

TSF refers to "Tribal Security Force." I will also employ the word Arbakai next to it, as this is the Afghan term most used to describe the type of tribal element our TETs would "advise, assist, train and lead."

I am not here to imply that I think I could win the war in Afghanistan if put in charge. Or that I can meet these challenges alone, or that there aren't soldiers out there who could do it better. I just know what I have done and what I could do again, if given the chance.

Fight Tactically —
Think Strategically

A SOLDIER'S JOURNEY
OF DISCOVERY

Anytime I receive instruction from anyone, listen to someone speak, or read an article written by someone, my first question always is: Who are you? Why is what you are saying relevant? What is your background? What are your experiences? What are you getting out of what you are doing or saying or selling?

So here are my answers to those questions. What do I consider my greatest military accomplishment? That I and the men I have trained and fought with have won twenty awards for valor. Twenty. That is a truly remarkable number. I had a great ODA (Operational Detachment Alpha) 316 in Afghanistan as part of the 3rd Special Forces Group. We fought together for several years in Afghanistan. We fought in the Konar and Helmand Provinces in early 2003 and again in 2004.

I then spent two years on a Special Projects team before returning to Iraq as the first American combat advisor for an Iraqi National Police Quick Reaction Force (QRF) battalion. Our mission was to kill and capture terrorists anywhere in the country. I won a Silver Star and the Iraqi National Police Medal of Honor while fighting alongside my Iraqi brothers in 2006 and 2007 when Iraq was the most dangerous place on earth.

I spent the next two years as an unconventional warfare (UW) instructor in the final phase of Special Forces training. After much red tape I was overjoyed to receive orders to return to Afghanistan in the summer of 2009 to once again spend time with the Afghan people and fight the Taliban. That is when I began writing this paper. A few days before leaving, I was informed that I would not be returning—I would be going to the 1st Armored Division to work on a transition team for a return trip to Iraq.

My experiences since 9/11 have been incredible. I have fought with great warriors against worthy enemies in both Iraq and Afghanistan. We fought with exceptional bravery and courage at every turn, but we always fought smartly and were always prepared for the challenges we faced.

This paper represents only a small portion of what ODA 316 accomplished in Afghanistan. It's my story of the tribal engagement between myself and Malik Noor Afzhal, my team and the rest of his tribe.

We must work first and forever with the tribes, for they are the most important military, political and cultural unit in that country. The tribes are self-contained fighting units who will fight to the death for their tribal family's honor and respect. Their intelligence and battlefield assessments are infallible. Their loyalty to family and friends is beyond question.

My unit and I became family members with Malik Noor Afzhal's tribe. This is my story of what we accomplished as a family in mutual respect and purpose. I'm offering our experience as a blueprint for success.

There is no doubt it could be done again.

Major Jim Gant
United States Army Special Forces

We demonstrated month in and month out that a small effective fighting force could unite with an Afghan tribe, become trusted and respected brothers-in-arms with their leaders and families, and make a difference in the US effort in Afghanistan. In doing so, we discovered what I believe to be the seed of enduring success in that country.

PROBLEMS, CHALLENGES, QUESTIONS

The following are issues beyond the scope of this paper that would have to be addressed and dealt with to accomplish the goals set forth in these pages. I cite them in this space, up front, so that the reader understands that I am aware of them and of their importance and difficulty. I will not attempt to address these issues in this paper. The time and research required are simply beyond my pay grade. By themselves, these issues demand papers or even books.

Beyond the strategy itself, what has to happen for a Tribal Engagement Strategy (TES) to work?

1. A strategy of tribal engagement will require a complete shift at the highest levels of our military organization— and the ability to push these changes down to group/brigade and battalion commanders. I believe Secretary Gates, General Petraeus and General McChrystal are flexible and forceful enough to embrace a strategy of this type. My fear is that the farther down the "food-chain" it travels, the more it might be resisted by ground commanders.

What specific tactical changes need to happen?

- **Command and Control of the Tribal Engagement Teams** (TETs) would have to be streamlined dramatically. "One radio call could get an answer."

- **The CONOP approval process** (used to get missions approved from higher headquarters has to be streamlined. Some missions might have to be conducted with no approval, due to the time-sensitive nature of the opportunity. The TETs would need special "trust and approval."

- **The risk-averse nature** of our current method of operating would have to change. American soldiers would die. Some of them alone, with no support. Some may simply disappear. Everyone has to understand that from the outset.

- **TETs must be allowed to be on their own**, grow beards, wear local garb, and interact with the tribesmen at all levels. They must be allowed to be what they are: "American tribesmen."

- **Use of OPFUND (money) needs to be streamlined.** The TETs will need special trust to do what is needed with money allocated to help the tribe. Money and guns equal the ultimate power.

- **Rules of Engagement (ROE) must change.** Using the TETs will become a very intense, personal fight. If they need to drop bombs or pursue an enemy, they must be able to do so. The teams will always fight alongside Tribal Security Forces (TSFs), and no missions will be conducted unilaterally. There will always be an Afghan face on any mission.

2. Identifying, attracting and training American personnel who could perform this type of mission would be a daunting task.

3. The strategic challenge of Pakistan as a sanctuary, recruiting base and source of funding and military expertise would have to be addressed. The United States

cannot afford to destabilize Pakistan any more than it already is. However, a TES (Tribal Engagement Strategy) could positively influence this situation. Most Taliban funding, recruitment and training takes place in Pakistan. Not to mention the safe haven it provides.

4. The lack of a viable judicial system. The current government-led judicial system is corrupt, slow and there are too few judges deemed legitimate by the populace to properly impose any rule of law in the vast and largely rural areas of Afghanistan. The Taliban has moved into many of these areas and gained footholds by dispensing justice, adjudicating disputes and acting as judges. It will take decades to improve this situation.

5. The warlord issue in Afghanistan. Do we fight them? Pay them? Co-opt them?

Use them as surrogates? Advise, assist and train them like we would do with the tribes? The warlords can definitely be used in a very effective surrogate role, in support of our objectives. We also need to understand that some fighters whom the US has labeled as "warlords" are really "environmentally-induced leaders" who fill a power vacuum of one type or another and that they would be very receptive to and even desirous of US assistance.

6. The opium problem. The tie between opium and the funding of the Taliban is a fact. However, at the tactical level, it would be a mistake for US forces to get involved in this issue. To do so would make enemies out of a population that is simply struggling to feed its families, clans and tribes. The COIN (counterinsurgency) forces should not be made responsible for the opium issue.

That would be counterproductive for the troops on the ground.

A strategy of tribal engagement will require a complete paradigm shift at the highest levels of our military organization.

So...what is the answer? My hope is that you will find it as you read through this paper.

You get a much different perspective on what this war means when you're in a tribal village. You look down at the children and see the hope and trust and anticipation in their eyes. It puts a little more fire in your belly to do something that really matters.

FOREWORD

*"Even if you take a Pashtun person
to paradise by force, he will not go.
He will go with you only
by friendly means."*

**– Inam-ur-Rahman, head of
the Swat Valley Peace Committee
in Pakistan**

Afghanistan. I feel like I was born there. The greatest days of my entire life were spent in the Pesch Valley and Musa Qalay and with the great "Sitting Bull" (a tribal leader in the Konar Valley) who you will meet later in these pages.

I love the people and the rich history of Afghanistan. They will give you their last bite of food in the morning and then try and kill you in the evening. A people who, despite their great poverty, are as happy as any American I have ever met. A people who will fight and die for the sake of honor. A great friend and a worthy enemy.

I have been asked by several people inside and outside of the military, "Who is your audience for this paper? What are you trying to accomplish?"

The answer is that I have been trying to get back to Afghanistan for several years, to Konar Province, to my old stomping grounds. In June of 2008 I received orders to return there on a transition team. I started this paper as an individual "IPb" or Intelligence Preparation of the battlefield. It began as my attempt to "wrap my brain around" the tribal issues that I knew my team and I would have to face.

I am writing this paper to help myself and possibly others determine how to best utilize the most powerful aspect of Afghan society—the tribes and the tribal system—not only to help the United States accomplish its strategic goals, but to help the Afghan people achieve peace, stability and good governance.

Afghan tribes always have and always will resist any type of foreign intervention in their affairs. This includes a central government located in Kabul, which to them is a million miles away from their problems, a million miles away from their security.

"Democracy" only has a chance to be cultivated at the local level by a small group of men—Tribal Engagement Teams—who are willing to dedicate their lives to the Afghan people and cause.

At a time when the outcome of the war in Afghanistan hangs in the balance, when high ranking military officers are asking for more troops, I believe the "light footprint" approach put forth in this paper will not only work, but will help to ease the need for larger and larger numbers of US soldiers being deployed to Afghanistan.

The central cultural fact about Afghanistan is that it is constituted of tribes. Not individuals, not Western-style citizens—but tribes and tribesmen. It is my deep belief—and the thesis of this paper—that the answer to the problems that face the Afghan people, as well as other future threats to US security in the region, will be found in understanding and then helping the tribal system of Afghanistan to flourish.

I firmly believe that a relatively small number of special officers and noncommissioned officers could maintain influence on large portions of Afghanistan by advising, assisting, training and leading local tribal security forces (Arbakai) and building strong relationships with the tribes they live alongside.

One Tribe at a Time reflects what I believe to be the one strategy that can help both the US and the people of Afghanistan by working directly with their centuries-old tribal system. We can only do this by giving top priority to the most important political, social and military force in Afghanistan— the tribes. We must engage these tribes at a close and personal level with a much deeper cultural understanding than we have ever had before.

When we gain the respect and trust of one tribe, in one area, a domino effect will spread throughout the region and beyond. One tribe will eventually become twenty-five or even fifty tribes. This can only have a long-term positive effect on the current situation. It is, however, not without pitfalls and difficulty.

But it can and must be done.

This is my vehicle after it hit an IED on the night of 24 Nov 2006 during my last tour in Iraq. The explosion flipped it three times and it was on fire when it landed. I was pinned inside and could not get out. I remember thinking, "So this is how it ends..." then I lost consciousness. My Iraqis somehow pulled me out and took care of me. Although I want to go back to Afghanistan so badly, I owe the Iraqis my life—and if they still need me, I feel obligated to go.

Afghan tribes always have and always will resist any type of foreign intervention in their affairs.

INTRODUCTION

The US has been in Afghanistan for eight years. We have fought hard and accomplished some good. Tactically, we have not lost a battle. Despite the lethal sophistication of the Improvised Explosive Device (IED) threat, we defeat the Taliban in every engagement. But are we closer to our goals than we were eight years ago? Are the Afghan people closer to a stable way of life? Are we closer to our national strategic objectives there?

Based on my time in Afghanistan—and my study of the region, tribes, counterinsurgency (COIN) and unconventional warfare (UW)—positive momentum in Afghanistan depends on the US forces' support for the tribal systems already in place. Take it a step further and "advise, assist, train and lead" tribal security forces (Arbakais) much like we have been doing with the Afghanistan National Army (ANA) and Afghanistan National Police (ANP).

I will get into the specifics later in this paper, but what I believe must happen is a tribal movement supported by the US which allows the tribal leaders and the tribes they represent to have access to the local, district, provincial, and national leadership. This process has to be a "bottom-up" approach.

There is no shortage of information detailing Afghan corruption at all levels of government. This directly affects the tribes. If the national government cannot protect "us," if US forces cannot protect "us," if we cannot protect ourselves…the only answer is to side with the Taliban. How can you blame anyone for that? I would do the same. As we all know, the answers to the problems in Afghanistan and Pakistan have no purely military answer. However, the political strategy of governing from Kabul or fighting the war from there is clearly not working. It never has. More importantly, it never will.

Afghanistan has never had a strong central government. A strategy in which the central government is the centerpiece of our counterinsurgency plan is destined to fail. It disenfranchises the very fabric of Afghan society. The tribal system in Afghanistan has taken a brutal beating for several decades. By supporting and giving some power back to the tribes, we can make positive progress in the region once again.

Even the people who advise our national policymakers see the need to engage the tribes. "The Afghan government is not competent enough to deal with the dire threats that currently face Afghanistan," says Seth Jones, an analyst at the RAND Corporation who advises the Pentagon. "This means working with tribal leaders." (Jones 2008, Sappenfield 2008)

I have fought on the battlefields of both Iraq and Afghanistan. Afghanistan is by far the more difficult and brutal operational environment. The enemy there has never been defeated. Time is on their side. Trust me. I have sat face to face with Afghans, both friends and enemies, who endure unimaginable hardships. They will do it, their children will do it and their children's children will do it. They own all the time.

When one says "Afghan people" what I believe they are really saying is "tribal member." Every single Afghan is a part of a tribe and understands how the tribe operates and why. This is key for us to understand. Understanding and operating within the tribe is the only way we can ever know who our friends and enemies are, how the Afghan people think and what is important to them. Because, above all, they are tribesmen first.

It is a matter of national security that the US government and specifically the military grasp the importance of the tribes and learn to operate comfortably in a tribal setting. This paper is about why and how we need to engage the tribal structure present in Afghanistan.

> *A strategy in which the central government is the centerpiece of our counterinsurgency plan is destined to fail. It disenfranchises the very fabric of Afghan society.*

1

DEFINING "WIN"

We have killed thousands and thousands of the "enemy" in Afghanistan and it clearly has not brought us closer to our objectives there. We could kill thousands more and still not be any closer five years from now.

Everyone talks about "winning" in Afghanistan. But what does that mean? The most current definition from President Obama is to "disrupt, dismantle, and defeat" the terrorist network, al-Qaeda in Afghanistan and Pakistan. More importantly, the president also added, "and to prevent the return of al-Qaeda in either country in the future."

Although a topic for another paper, US forces in Afghanistan have accomplished that mission and could continue to do so until our national or political will to stay there runs out—and everyone knows this time is quickly approaching.

We cannot make progress in Afghanistan through a war of attrition or a war of exhaustion. As I have said and will continue to say, time is on their side. In an insurgency, all the insurgents have to do is not lose. All they have to do is wear down the will of the counterinsurgent and in this case, the will of the American people and the American politicians.

Either approach (attrition or exhaustion) will not work. We have killed thousands and thousands of the "enemy" in Afghanistan and it clearly has not brought us closer to our objectives there. Just as important is the fact that we could kill thousands more and still not be any closer five years from now.

JIM GANT

My definition of "success" (that is, "win") includes the one currently in use. I would add: "…to facilitate security and prosperity for the Afghan people." In other words, the tribes.

We will be totally unable to protect the "civilians" in the rural areas of Afghanistan until we partner with the tribes for the long haul. Their tribal systems have been there for centuries and will be there for many more. Why should we fight against not only what they have been accustomed to for centuries, but what works for them? They will not change their tribal ways. And why should they?

Bottom Line

"Winning" in Afghanistan will be an elusive prospect until we base our operations within the cultural framework of the tribal systems already in place.

2

WE ARE LOSING THE WAR IN AFGHANISTAN

The former military commander in charge of Afghanistan, General David McKiernan, said in March 2009, "The coalition is not winning the war against the resurgent Taliban in certain parts of the country." (Cowell 2009)

Afghanistan has never had a strong central government and never will. That is a fact that we need to accept, sooner rather than later.

Time and US popular support is the strategic center of gravity (COG) for US forces.

Time and the population of not only Afghanistan but Pakistan is the strategic COG for the Taliban.

Using the old "find out what is important to your enemy and destroy it, and know what is important to you and protect it" won't work in the current fight in Afghanistan. Make no mistake, the people (or politicians) of the US will get tired of the war and will eventually make the US military pull out.

Time is not on our side considering the current level of blood and treasure that we are expending. A war of exhaustion is unacceptable and a war of annihilation is not feasible. We do not have the patience or the resources to stay on our current course.

The sophistication of Taliban attacks in Afghanistan has risen in the last two years to a point where we can clearly see that they will continue to adapt to our strategies and tactics.

The US also is losing the information battle. We do not get our message out as effectively as the Taliban does. Our tactical PSYOP (Psychological Operations) is not responsive enough to make the impact we need at the small unity level.

Recruitment for the Taliban is not waning; it is in fact increasing. The US has killed tens of thousands of "insurgents" in Afghanistan, but we are no closer to victory today than we were in 2002.

Pakistan, and in particular, the Federally Administered Tribal Areas (FATA) and the Northwest Frontier Provinces (NWFP) will play a major role in the success or failure of the US counterinsurgency (COIN) effort in Afghanistan, as well as the overall stability of the region. These "ungoverned areas" in Pakistan are among the few areas where al-Qaeda needs to maintain some amount of physical control so they can train and plan in safety. Why is this important? Because these areas are tribal in nature. As I will describe later in the paper, many of the tribes in eastern Afghanistan straddle these border regions. If we can influence the entire tribe on both sides of the border, the US can have greater influence in the entire region.

I like using analogies. If the war in Afghanistan is a boxing match, here's what's happening: The US has won every round but has not been able to knock them (Taliban) out. The fight has no limit on the number of rounds that can be fought. We will continue to punish them, but never win the fight. It will go on indefinitely or until we (the US) grow tired and quit.

The only existing structure that offers governance and security for the Afghan people is at the tribal level. We should leverage this and use it to our advantage—before it is too late.

Bottom Line:

We are losing the war in Afghanistan because, simply put, we are not "winning." All the Taliban has to do is not lose.

We've got the watches, but they've got the time.

– Army saying in Afghanistan

3

TRIBES UNDERSTAND PEOPLE, PROTECTION, POWER AND PROJECTION

First, tribes understand people. Being illiterate does not mean unintelligent. Tribesmen are extremely adept at understanding one another and others. As I have preached and preached to the Special Forces officers headed to Afghanistan that I have trained in the unconventional warfare (UW) portion of their training, "You damn well better know yourself because they know you." The Afghan people have a knack for looking straight through deception and incompetence.

Trust me when I tell you, not only are they as smart as you are, they know they are.

Second, tribes understand protection. Tribes are organized and run to ensure the security of the tribe. Not only physical security, but revenue and land protection. But most important of all is the preservation of the tribal name and reputation. Honor is everything in a tribal society. Tribes will fight and die over honor alone (I will speak more about this later). This concept is not understood by a vast majority of strategists who are trying to find solutions to challenges we are facing in Afghanistan.

When honor is at stake, tribal members stop at nothing to preserve their tribe's integrity and "face."

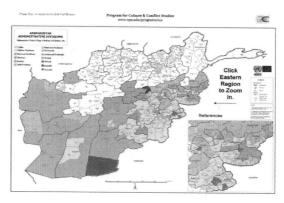

Tribes are the most important aspect of Afghan
society and have been for centuries.

Third, tribes understand power. How many
guns do we have? How many warriors can
I put in the field? Can I protect my tribe?
Can I attack others who threaten my tribe?
Can I back my words or decisions up with
the ability to come down the valley and kill
you? Can I keep you from killing me?

Lastly, tribes understand projection. Tribes
have no "strategic goals" in the Western
sense. Their diplomatic, informational,

military and economic (DIME) priorities are almost without exception in reference to other tribes.

Can I project my power across the valley? Does the tribe across the river know not to come over here and meddle in my affairs? Does the Taliban know that they are not welcome here? Can I influence decisions, either by force or otherwise, outside of my tribe?

Tribes offer their members security, safety, structure and significance. What other institutions do that right now in Afghanistan?

"Tribes," says RAND Senior Fellow David Ronfeldt in his paper, "Tribes—The First and Forever Form," "can foster a sense of social solidarity. [Belonging to a tribe] fills people with pride and self-respect. It motivates families to protect, welcome and care for each other and to abide by strict rituals that affirm their connections as tribal members to their ancestors, land and deity. This kinship creates trust and loyalty in which one knows and must uphold one's rights, duties and obligations. What maintains order in a tribe is mutual respect, dignity, pride and honor."

Tribes by nature are conservative. They hate change and they don't change. "The more tribal the society, the more resistant it will be to change." (Ronfeldt 2006, 73). The tribal system has been the means of governance in Central Asia for centuries. It has resisted and defeated invaders since Cyrus the Great. The more an alien force tries to change the way tribes live, the more the tribes resist.

"What maintains order in a tribe is not hierarchy and law, but a code that stresses mutual respect, dignity, pride, and honor."

-David Ronfeldt, "Tribes— The First and Forever Form"

What about democracy? A tribe is a "natural democracy." In Afghan shuras and jirgas (tribal councils), every man's voice has a chance to be heard. The fact that women and minority groups have no say in the process does not make it less effective nor less of a democracy to them. Asking them to change the way they have always conducted their business through their jirgas and shuras just does not make sense.

We need to integrate ourselves into the process as trusted "advisors" to the tribal leadership. They need to know that we have their best interests in mind. The strengths that these tribal organizations show can be used eventually to establish cooperation and political integration with the central government (more than likely not our model, but a type). This would take time.

Bottom Line:

We must support the tribal system because it is the single, unchanging political, social and cultural reality in Afghan society and the one system that all Afghans understand, even if we don't. We must also remember that the Pashtun tribes are fighting to preserve a centuries-old way of life.

Tribes offer their members security, safety, structure and significance. What other institutions do that right now in Afghanistan?

4

MY PERSONAL EXPERIENCE WITH A TRIBE IN KONAR PROVINCE

My entire premise is based on my experience with tribal engagement in Konar Province in 2003 with ODA 316, of which I was the team leader.

First, I hesitate to write this chapter for purely personal reasons. I have not acted alone. I had a great ODA with outstanding warriors and NCOs. This is not a story about the bravery, valor or camaraderie that we showed every single day—together. This is but one aspect of the overall mission we accomplished as a team. I will only write from my own perspective and will not attempt to speak for any other team members.

Program for Culture and Conflict Studies

MOHMAND

Also, there are aspects of this portion of the mission that cannot be told in this forum for many reasons. I will leave it at that.

A few points before I describe the relationship my men and I built with the village of Mangwel in Konar Province.

First, I am unable to tell the entire story for operational reasons that include some of the missions we did together (with the tribes) and some of the tactics, techniques and procedures involved in doing so. I am also concerned about the safety of the tribesmen who helped us so very much.

Second, the trip to and from our MSS (Mission Support Site) or FB (Fire Base) in Asadabad to Mangwel was a life-threatening event. It was a combat patrol that, more often than not, encountered enemy contact somewhere along the way, and in several cases there were multiple contacts.

Third, the tribe offered us outstanding intelligence that allowed us to target both insurgents and terrorists in the area. Their loyalty was with us. Not Afghan forces or US forces, but us.

Lastly, I will only write about a few of the major events that took place. The entire story is a book. The primary point here is that I was able to have "influence without authority" in this area through the tribal leadership and its great leader, whom we came to call "Sitting Bull."

ODA 316 deployed to Asadabad in Konar Province in April 2003. We got off a helicopter in the middle of the night having nothing but the broad mission statement of "kill and capture anti-coalition members." I am not sure that there was an overall plan or strategy for Afghanistan at the time. We were making it up as we went along. The tactical reality was that we were fighting for our lives every single day.

We were safer in Mangwel than we were in our own firebase in Asadabad.

Our First Encounter with a Tribal Leader

The immediate imperative was to get a feel for the area, to gather intelligence and to meet with as many village elders as possible. To accomplish this, I planned to conduct multiple Armed Reconnaissance patrols. Basically we were announcing our presence and inviting contact, friendly or hostile. On our second mission, we were attacked in a well-planned RPG ambush. We fought our way out and moved on to a small village in Khas Khonar, where we were told there was a "problem" in another village called Mangwel. We moved to Mangwel and we were met there by a man named Akhbar, the village doctor.

I got out my laptop and showed Malik Noor Afzhal video footage of the World Trade Center towers collapsing. He had never seen this and it made a deep impression.

After some negotiations, the doctor and some of the other elders said they would get their leader. Soon afterward, Malik (tribal leader) Noor Afzhal came into the compound. I was immediately aware of his presence and the respect that he carried with him. He invited several of my teammates and me in to sit down and drink some tea and talk. I made it a point to relax and put my weapon to the side.

Dr. Akhbar is the first person we met in Mangwel.

After introducing one another, he asked why we were there. Why had armed Americans come to his country? We spoke for some two hours. I got out my laptop and showed Malik Noor Afzhal video footage of the World Trade Center towers collapsing. He had never seen this and it made a deep impression. He had heard about 9/11 and now understood that we were there to fight the Taliban and al-Qaeda.

He then asked me why other US forces had passed through his village but had never stopped to talk with him. I explained that I could not speak for other US soldiers, but only for me and my men.

An important note here: I could feel that he and I were very comfortable with one another soon after we began talking. I spent a lot of time just listening. I spoke only when I thought I understood what had been said. My questions mostly pertained to things he had said, to ensure I had an understanding of what he was intending to say. I had a very good interpreter so this was made easier. The fact that my interpreter was middle-aged, well-educated and a Pashtun was invaluable.

The malik then asked us to stay for lunch, which I immediately agreed to.

After a great lunch, we began to speak again. The malik spoke about the problems he was having in his village. The one that concerned him most was a bad situation within his own tribe. I will not get into the specifics of the different clans and sub-clans but there was a "highland" people and a "lowland" people.

Noor Afzhal's tribe included people whose physical location is on both sides of the Afghanistan-Pakistan border. The highlands people had taken and were using some land that belonged to the lowland people. The malik told me the land had been given to his tribe by the "King of Afghanistan" many, many years ago and that he would show me the papers.

Dining with the tribe in Mangwel. I'm sitting second
from the left next to my interpreter, across from Scott
Gross' nose and Tony Siriwardene to his right. Sitting
Bull is standing in the background smiling.

Afghan food is delicious. For the first several months
in Asadabad, the tribe fed us the only fresh vegetables
we ever ate. We ate three meals a day with them and
never was there a bad one. I was amazed because the
people had so little, but they shared the best they had
with us. Most often we ate lamb with a spicy pepper
sauce, fresh tomatoes and onions. Bread and rice
were the main staples. Each meal ended with some
type of sweet made of nuts or fruit.

After the second time they fed us, I asked my
interpreter if I could pay them for the meal. He told
me I could not do that. I then began to understand
melmastia, the tribal imperative of hospitality that is
used by the Pashtuns. I quickly figured out other ways
to "pay" them for their hospitality.

I told him he didn't need to show me any papers. His word was enough.

He then told me he had given the highlanders ten days to comply with the request or he and his men would retake it by force. Here was the critical point for me and my relationship with Malik Noor Afzhal.

It is hard on paper to explain the seriousness of the situation and the complexity we both were facing. He had asked for help, a thing he later would tell me was hard for him to do (especially from an outsider) and I had many options. Could I afford to get involved in internal tribal warfare? What were the consequences if I did? With the tribe? With the other tribes in the area? With my own chain of command?

I made the decision to support him. "Malik, I am with you. My men and I will go with you and speak with the highlanders again.

If they do not turn the land back over to you, we will fight with you against them." With that, a relationship was born. Malik Noor Afzhal then told me he had only eight warriors on duty at the current time. I told him, "No, you have sixteen." (I had eight team members at the time).

We talked for hours, discussing what next steps to take. Then, out of the blue the malik leaned over and told my interpreter to tell me that he had not been completely honest, that he had not eight, but eighty warriors. I looked back at the malik, smiled and nodded my head in approval.

A lot more tea was drunk and a lot more information was exchanged, none of which I can talk about but all of which went toward deepening the bond between ODA 316 and the malik and his tribe. It was getting late. Noor Afzhal told my interpreter that he needed to speak with me alone, outside. He took my hand, looked me in the eye and said, "Commander Jim, I have eight hundred warriors and they are at your disposal. You only need to ask and they will be yours."

"Jim, the last time I saw a person with a face like yours [white] the Russians killed eighty-six men, women and children of my village... They never took my village. We are ready to fight again if we have to. You have great warriors with you. We will fight together."

– Malik Noor Afzhal (Sitting Bull)

From eight to eighty to eight hundred. Without going into further detail, suffice it to say that the dispute with the highlanders was resolved. And we of ODA 316 had learned two lessons about Tribal

Engagement that, if anything, are more important today than they were then.

We saw firsthand the depth and power of the existing (though invisible to us) tribal defense system. And we grasped the absolute necessity of working with and bonding with the tribal leader—man to man, warrior to warrior.

We Bond with the Village, "One Tribe to Another"

Maybe a Special Forces ODA can understand an Afghan tribe because we ourselves are a tribe. And the Afghans recognize this. As time went by and we fought in many ambushes and engagements throughout the river valley and around other villages, the tribe came to believe that we were on their side and that we had come to help. With this, they began to open up to us. Here's one example:

JIM GANT

Our team was in Mangwel. Malik Noor
Afzhal asked us to stay the night as we had
many topics to discuss. Was this safe? I
quickly counted over sixty armed warriors
providing security. There were sentries high
in the mountains (on the Pakistani side) that
we were not meant to see, and three layers
of security near the malik's compound. We
set up a hasty defensive perimeter (HDP)
with our vehicles and got settled. The malik
then approached me and said he wanted to
take me somewhere very special.

I, of course, agreed. I grabbed three of my
men, we got in several pick-up trucks with
Malik Noor Afzhal and his men, and began
traveling up towards the beautiful mountain
range behind Mangwel (with just weapons,
no body armor) towards Pakistan. We drove
up a valley and past an Afghan cemetery
with many large flat rocks emplaced into
the ground. We noticed many graves. Off
in the distance, what appeared to be an old
village had been destroyed.

The vehicles parked and we all got out, Malik Noor Afzhal grabbed my hand and we walked hand in hand up a small valley into the mountains. We turned at a small bend and there was a beautiful waterfall. He told us to drink the water.

He then came next to me and said (through my interpreter), "Jim, the last time I saw a person with a face like yours (meaning white) the Russians killed eighty-six men, women and children of my village."

He continued, "This is my old village. We fought the Russians. They never took my village. We are ready to fight again if we have to." He looked and finished with, "You have great warriors with you. We will fight together."

We stood there for a few minutes and looked back into the valley, where you could see the old village and the new one. It was a remarkable moment that cannot be put into any metrics or computer program that defines "success" today. But it was. The bond continued to grow.

Below is a photo that captured that moment, as we were about to leave.

This was taken just before Sitting Bull took me up to "Old Mangwel," his old village the Russians had destroyed. Fifth from the left is Sitting Bull holding my M-4 with me at his side. My team member standing is SFC Travis Weitzel. Kneeling in front of me is SFC Mark Read and far right kneeling is SFC Scott Gross. We handed our weapons over to them for the photo.

It was also this night where, in great detail, I explained to Malik Noor Afzhal why we referred to him as "Sitting Bull." He was not only captivated by the story of this great

American Indian warrior and leader of his people, but it was a great honor to him that we viewed him in that way.

I want to interject a couple of situations that might also tell of the relationship that was built with Malik Noor Afzhal and my team. He and Dr. Akhbar were very open with their homes and families. I spent countless hours playing with Dr. Akhbar's small children and the malik's grandchildren and great grandchildren. The malik used to say to me, "Jim, I am getting too old. Play with the children today. They love you." So do you know what my primary task would be for the day? I would play with the children—for hours.

The little girls and I would walk around the village holding hands and laughing at "stuff." They would teach me Pashto and I would teach them English. We would be watched by literally hundreds of younger children and women as we played. I often thought that these play sessions did more for our cause in Konar than all the raids we did combined.

Their families became our families

Playing with the kids. A lot of trust was built between my team and the tribe by the way we treated their children.

Another very enjoyable, insightful and important part of our conversations was discussing the war against the Soviets with the malik and his men. I cannot tell you how much I enjoyed it and learned from it. The tribesmen loved to explain in detail, to us and in front of each other, their great exploits on the battlefield against "the Bear."

One of Sitting Bull's mujahedeen commanders describes ambush tactics they used against the Soviets. I loved these sessions and I learned a lot. The tribesmen enjoyed being able to tell us stories of their great battles.

My men developed their own personal and professional relationships with the people. Each one had his own following. When we would drive up to the village, different sets of children, young people and elders would run up to different members of the team, calling them by name.

Here is a brief quote from Captain Dan McKone, my medic and gunner during my time in the Konar. He has won three awards for valor. No warrior understands Afghanistan better than he does. (He is there now advising the ANA):

> *Mangwel was a high point in my time as a soldier, no doubt. Our team's (ODA 316) ability to connect and establish a relationship based on friendship and trust has yet to be replicated...and it sounds like the army is not going to try it again. I remember strongly, that for me, I felt that we wanted to develop cooperation, not*

dependence. This was very true for me and my relationship with Dr. Akhbar. We, as a team, wanted to support him and, of course, through him add to Sitting Bull's ability to provide for his people more than just promises, to show concrete dividends for having a positive friendship with an outside force. As Dr. Akhbar ran a for-profit clinic in the village, and appeared to have credibility as the village doctor, we could not do anything to undercut his credibility, or his ability to make a living. How things would have panned out over a longer period of time would have been great to see. Alas, it was not to be.

Then SSG McKone's relationship with Dr. Akhbar was a key to our team's success in Mangwel. Dan's now a captain and winner of three awards for valor.

*In between or Armed Reconnaisance patrols and
operations with Sitting Bull's warriors, we experienced
the exact opposite of war with the tribe's children. In
short, they loved us and we loved them. A big bright
spot was when several hundred dollars' worth of
toys arrived from my wife and other members of my
team's families. It was a happy holiday for the kids and
everyone else in the village. The smiles on their faces
made us all the more honored to be there. I'm in the
top photo with Sitting Bull and a happy girl. Below, my
team and I were at the girls' school handing out much
needed supplies.*

Not All Fun and Games

While all of this was going on, we were getting an amazing amount of actionable intelligence from Malik Noor Afzhal's intelligence people, his kasheeka. We received a lot of information from locals at our firebase on a daily basis, but most of it was worthless. The information we got from Malik Noor Afzhal and his men was correct one hundred percent of the time. Their intelligence nets and early-warning systems were superior.

For example, my ODA was engaged in a significant enemy contact in the late evening in the summer of 2003 in the Pesch Valley, about twenty-five kilometers north of our firebase and sixty kilometers from Mangwel. The very next morning at around 0800, Dr. Akhbar and several other elders came to our firebase to check on us as they had heard we were attacked.

When I asked them how they had found out, they simply answered, "Word travels quickly here."

My Biggest Regret

Over time, it became very clear that the relationship we had built with the tribe was causing them to become a target for HIG (warlord Gulbuddin Hekmatyar's armed party, Hezb-e Islami) in the area. We could not stay in the village twenty-four hours a day due to our other mission requirements.

74

In retrospect and with many more years of experience under my belt, not setting up our base in Mangwel was a mistake.

Dr. Akhbar and a few tribal members came to check up on us after our firebase came under attack the night before.

Since we could not maintain a twenty-four-hour presence in the village (which they had asked for on two separate occasions), I decided to give them as many weapons and as much ammo as I could get my hands on. I felt like not only was it the best thing to do, but the moral thing to do as well. I had asked them to risk so much—what else was I supposed to do?

I am comfortable with the decision for two reasons. First, the tribe needed more weapons to help defend themselves and, more importantly, Malik Noor Afzhal and his people viewed these weapons as great gifts. These were gifts not only of honor but trust as well. These gifts bound us together even more than we already were. Power in this area was about the ability to put armed men on the ground to attack an adversary or defend their tribe. Guns were the ultimate currency.

A principal tenet of the One Tribe at a Time concept is that US Trial Engagement Teams "advise, assist, train and lead" the tribal forces they are paired with. Under "assist," we need to add "arm and supply." I will have more to say about this in Chapter 8: How to Engage the Tribes.

The last time we visited Mangwel, Sitting Bull and Dr. Akhbar's wives gave me beautiful, hand-made jewelry to specifically give to my wife and daughter. As they handed me these gifts, they told me, "Thank you for what you have done for us. Thank your wife for sending our children gifts." The jewelry is beautiful, but what it represents means the most.

Bottom Line

We were safer in Mangwel than on our own firebase. The relationships we built there are still reaping dividends in the Konar region, more than six years after we left.

See "Gifts of Honor" on Steven Pressfield's website at http://blog.stevenpressfield.com.

5

PASHTUNWALI AND ITS TACTICAL APPLICATIONS

Pashtunwali is the code of honor the Pashtun tribes live by. Understanding it is crucial if one is going to learn about or become part of a Pashtun tribe.

The law, as we understand it in the West, is not the basis for the tribal societies. That function is performed by a code of honor. It has been my experience that many Western soldiers—officers and NCOs alike—do not perceive or understand "honor" as an Afghan does. Most Americans view honor as a mixture of honesty, integrity, respect, fairness and loyalty to one's country. In many ways the tribesmen I have dealt with think of honor in similar terms—as loyalty, courage, the ability to defend themselves, their families and their tribal communities.

But the tribesman is less concerned about "country"—which for him is almost irrelevant—and more concerned about protecting the domain of his family, his customs, his tribal leadership, his warrior pride. He lives in a regional world where day-to-day military strength means the difference between survival and being overrun by other tribal elements whoever they might be (the Taliban, other aggressive tribes, or the Russian army).

There is no larger government force available to intervene and protect him when his tribe is in danger.

"Thus, warlords and warriors fighting in Afghanistan, Iraq and other tribal zones today are renowned for the value they place on upholding codes of honor and avoiding shameful humiliation. All want to gain honor for themselves and their lineage, clan and tribe. No one can afford to lose face, for that would reflect badly not only on them as individuals but also their kin. If the word were in the dictionary, it might be said that tribes and clans are deeply honoritarian." (Ronfeldt 2006, 35)

A "warrior code" is the centerpiece of the majority of tribal men, young and old, that I have known on a personal level. This code and their conception of honor is the tribe's collective center of gravity, as well as each individual's.

Sitting Bull and I often spoke of warriors. ODA 316 and I had proved ourselves in combat to them. It was this ability and opportunity to prove our physical courage to the tribesman that made them truly respect us.

The only other aspects of Pashtunwali I will mention are revenge (badal) and the hospitality (melmastia). The revenge aspect of the tribe in Mangwel was a real and tangible issue. It was interesting to me that this revenge aspect could be put into motion by the mere perception of challenging the tribe's honor or name. When, at one point, members of the Hezb-e Islami (HIG) accused Malik Noor Afzhal of letting Christianity be spread in his village, we both knew and understood this was a lie. However, it was the issue of his tribe's honor that caused our combined reaction of violence towards HIG.

"Principles of mutual respect, dignity, pride, and honor are so important in tribal societies that humiliating insults may upset peace and order more than anything else. An insult to an individual is normally regarded as an insult to all who belong to that lineage. Then there are only two ways to alleviate the sense of injury: compensation or revenge. And a call for compensation or revenge may apply not just to the offering individual but to his or her lineage. Responsibility is collective, and justice is less about inflicting punishment for a crime than about gaining adequate compensation or revenge to restore honor. It is not unusual to find clans and tribes engaged in prolonged cycles of reconciliation and revenge; i.e., fusion and fission deriving from insults that happened long ago." (Ronfeldt 2006, 39)

I would also be remiss if I did not mention the simply remarkable hospitality that we were shown every single time we visited Mangwel. The people always gave the very best of everything they had. They treated us with respect, dignity, and honor in every way, every single time we were together.

"The tribal form, at its best, embodies high ideals about how a society should be organized and how people should treat each other. Today, as in ancient times, social ideals about egalitarianism, mutual caring, sharing, reciprocity, collective responsibility, group solidarity, family, community, civility, and democracy all hark back to tribal principles." (Ronfeldt 2006, 59)

The honor of an Afghan woman can never be compromised. It sounds contrary to how they treat their women, but that is the point. Their world is one of contradictions (to outsiders) and is very hard to understand.

A personal point on this. I was invited inside the inner rooms of compounds in Mangwel on two occasions. Both times I was presented with gifts from the wives of two separate village elders. Neither time was even my interpreter allowed to go inside. Both times the wife was uncovered and personally handed me the gifts to give to my own wife and daughter.

Hearts and Minds vs. Shame and Honor

Pashtunwali has a definite effect on the tactics, techniques and procedures used, not only to fight the insurgency but to get the local population on our side. The Pashtun tribes will fight any and all outsiders, and refuse to accept being ruled by a central government.

An important tribal concept that the Tribal Engagement Teams must internalize is: "Hearts and Minds vs. Shame and Honor."

> A "warrior code" is the centerpiece of the majority of tribal men, young and old, that I have known on a personal level. This code and their conception of honor is the tribe's collective center of gravity, as well as each individual's.

The Pashtun can go from brother to mortal enemy—in sixty seconds. It is one of the things I respect and enjoy most about the Pashtun culture.

It is also important to remember that most of the insurgents are Pashtuns. In many cases the Taliban rule of law (Sharia law) is in direct conflict with Pashtunwali. We currently are not using this to our advantage.

Ask a Pashtun what comes first, Islam or Pashtunwali, and he will invariably answer: "Pashtunwali." (Malkasian and Meyerle 2009)

"The Pashtun people are unusual in the sense that they will willingly do things if asked respectfully, but will refuse point-blank if ordered to do so or threatened by force. Bombings and missile strikes won't force them to beg for mercy or cooperate with their attackers. They are made of sterner stuff. Their patience is endless and is borne out by their suffering during the past three decades." (Yusufzai)

Bottom Line:

A thorough and deep understanding and respect for Pashtunwali is critical for the success of US Tribal Engagement Teams and the overall US strategy in Afghanistan.

6

SIX PROBLEMS WITH CURRENT COIN STRATEGY AND ITS APPLICATION IN AFGHANISTAN

RAND recently published a detailed and informative book, *Counterinsurgency in Afghanistan*, by Seth Jones. It includes an analysis of ninety insurgencies since 1945. The study identifies three major variables correlated with the success and failure of the counterinsurgency efforts.

- Capability of indigenous security forces, especially police

- Local governance

- External support for insurgents, including sanctuary

David Kilcullen has echoed this in a White House briefing in 2008. The Taliban, he declared, has outfought and outthought us on all three critical fronts: "We have failed to secure the Afghan people. We have failed to deal with the sanctuary in Pakistan. The Afghan government does not deliver legitimate, good governance to Afghans at the local level." (Kilcullen 2008)

What We're Doing Now

Counterinsurgency strategy is rightly predicated on this primary objective: to "secure the population where they sleep." But how?

Right now, this effort has come entirely from the Kabul government, either through US forces or through the Afghan National Army (ANA) and Afghan National Police (ANP).

"The development of Afghan Security Forces has been a badly managed, grossly understaffed and poorly funded mess," says Anthony Cordesman, analyst at the Center for Strategic and International Studies. (Moreau and Yousafzai 2009, 33)

Current policy is to pour more time, money and resources into the ANA and ANP. We have been doing this for eight years now and what do we have? The ANA and ANP are symbols of the central government, which at present is not trusted by the tribes.

Yet we continue to stake the success of our mission on their development. We should continue to develop the will and capacity of the ANA and ANP, while simultaneously preparing the tribes to defend themselves.

As Defense Secretary Robert Gates recently said, "My worry is that the Afghans come to see us as part of the problem, rather than

part of the solution. And then we are lost."
(Moreau and Yousafzai 2009, 32)

The current program to train Afghan police is understaffed, under-resourced and full of corruption. Most importantly, the tribes' reluctance to accept any outside influence automatically qualifies them as one of the few viable options available to protect the population. Why continue to work against the tribal structures and traditions already in place? Not only let the tribes protect themselves, but encourage it.

How a Tribal Engagement Strategy (TES) Provides Security

Following the "Clear – Hold – Build" model, a small number of US TETs (Tribal Engagement Teams) —given enough time to train a Tribal Security Force (TSF) and the ability to call for US air support and aerial re-supply and a US Quick Reaction Force in an emergency—could conduct the "hold and build" portion of this strategy with a very limited footprint.

"A man with a gun rules a hundred without one."

– Vladimir Lenin

We are talking about the tribes providing security for themselves, with the assistance of the US Tribal Engagement Teams.

Security at the local (tribal) level is the key to security and support at the national level. No political change will ever take place without true security at the tribal level. A Tribal Engagement Strategy can help do that.

"We should consider how our counterinsurgency strategies and policies might include non-state groups in a civilian policing role. Scholars and analysts have observed that "third forces"—militias, private military companies, and even criminal organizations—can sometimes be opted to play useful counterinsurgency roles. These irregular forces might be induced to provide police-like protection to the civilian population." (Rosenau 2008, 22)

"If it is accepted that a major problem of the counterinsurgency in Afghanistan is the ability to control the villages, a logical conclusion would be that the formation of village militias is necessary." (Giustozzi 2008, 173)

Tribal militias also would inhibit the Taliban's ability to attack tribal members (the TSFs/Arbakai). With our Tribal Engagement Team (TET) support, the tribes could retaliate in strength against the Taliban.

Training and building relationships with the leaders of the tribe will be permanent fixes in large areas of rural Afghanistan. We will be able to stay there for the long haul with very little support once the systems are in place and the Tribal Security Forces (Arbakai) are well-trained and we have gained their trust. Trust in the tribe I worked with in Mangwel was worth everything.

> *The natural governance of Afghanistan is tribal. Through its councils, jirgas and shuras, tribal members have been dispensing justice and providing the means of conflict resolution for centuries.*

How a tribal Engagement Strategy Promotes Good Governance

The natural governance of Afghanistan is tribal. Through its councils, jirgas and shuras, tribal members have been dispensing justice and providing the means of conflict resolution for centuries. However, such traditional tribal mechanisms have been weakened by brutal and deliberate campaigns of assassination, intimidation, and co-optation—first by the Soviets, then the warlords, now by the Taliban.

"No one is currently doing the job of actual policing and enforcing the rule of law, keeping the population safe from all corners—including friendly fire and coalition operations, providing justice and dispute resolution, and civil and criminal law enforcement." (Kilcullen 2008)

Tribal Security Forces could do this through the tribal jirga system, beneath the authority of a tribal council and backed up by a Tribal Engagement Team to bring US resources, leadership and training to bear. Together with the tribal elders, they can act as peacemakers and brokers, bringing the important actors to negotiate.

These traditional institutions can facilitate justice and legitimacy through a local approach to resolving conflicts.

The Taliban…have been working in the villages for years to establish "shadow governments" of Sharia law courts and other indigenous institutions, providing the justice and fair play that the villagers cannot get from a remote and corrupt national government.

The Taliban know this, even if we don't. They have been working in the villages for years to establish "shadow governments" of Sharia law courts and other indigenous institutions, providing the justice and fair play that the villagers cannot get from a remote and corrupt national government.

"On a national scale, we are not going to win hearts or change minds. This must be done on the ground, person-to-person, by gaining respect and trust with each tribe. In other words, we need to employ a Tactical Engagement Strategy, one tribe at a time. Study and gain a detailed appreciation of Pashtunwali, the honor code of the

Pashtuns, in order to communicate effectively, whether kinetic or non-kinetic, within the target audience's cultural frame of reference." (McCallister 2008)

Speaking of Iraq, Carter Malkasian and Jerry Meyerle state, "Another way to reduce government misrule could be... to empower traditional tribal structures that may be more representative and have greater authority on the ground."

"In Afghanistan, tribes are even more important. Most Pashtuns identify themselves first and forever with their tribe, sub-tribe, or clan. Competing political institutions and figures are much weaker and most of the population lives in rural areas, far from government institutions." (Malkasian and Meyerle 2009)

Another major COIN tenet is to separate the insurgent from the population. The presence of the Tribal Engagement Teams would facilitate this very quickly. Once the TETs were on the ground with the tribal leadership, insurgent elements would either be killed or have to leave the area. The presence of the TETs would also make it difficult for the local Taliban supporters to be mobilized when the Taliban wanted to surge in certain areas.

Local Taliban fighters would be much more inclined to re-integrate into the tribe once the TSFs (Arbakai) start to be implemented. Which low-level Taliban members could re-integrate would, of course, be up to the tribal leadership.

Good governance is the follow-on to reliable security. Tribal Security Forces can facilitate both. "Unless you are confident in the ability of your government to enforce its peace, then the man with a gun at your door at midnight is your master." (Kelly 2009, 5)

How a Tribal Engagement Strategy Interdicts External Support for Insurgents

The safe-haven issue in the eastern and southern portion of Afghanistan is a huge factor that could potentially cause the failure of the entire campaign. From my own experience, the location and demographics of the village of Mangwel and members of the tribe located there make this a situation where we could and did acquire much more intelligence to make more informed decisions in that region.

Given enough time, effort and resources, a Tribal Engagement Strategy could be expanded to the entire border region, not only policing the infiltration routes from Pakistan (which the tribesmen know as intimately as we know the streets of our own hometown), but providing actionable intelligence about who has crossed over, where they are, and what potential danger they represent.

"Unless you are confident in the ability of your government to enforce its peace, then the man with a gun at your door at midnight is your master."

**– Justin Kelly,
How to win in Afghanistan**

Putting US soldiers (TETs) on the ground with the tribes will say more about our commitment than anything else we can do.

"US military operations most succeeded when leaders at the small-unit level had enough leeway, specialized assets, and firepower to engage the population and develop their own intelligence. Indeed, US military doctrine needs to establish far looser and more broadly distributed networks that have a high degree of independence and survivability. (Jones 2008, 98)

The RAND study also points out four more reasons to depend on indigenous actors to fight the war:

1. Most insurgencies have taken between eleven and fourteen years to win. Therefore, the indigenous forces eventually will have to win the war on their own, and they must develop the capacity to do so.

For some of our missions we dressed in Afghan garb, especially when we didn't want the Taliban to know our teams were operating in certain areas. Here I'm in the local garb with AK-47 ready to go. This is my favorite personal photo from Afghanistan.

2. Indigenous forces usually know the population and terrain better than external actors and are better able to gain intelligence.

3. A lead US role can be interpreted by the population as occupation (especially in Afghanistan).

4. A lead indigenous role can provide a focus for national aspirations and show the population that they control their own destiny.

Integrating Tribal Security Forces into the National Security Apparatus

These Tribal Security Forces should be used to assist—not replace—the national and local police.

The bond here between the tribal leaders and councils and their US counterparts on the Tribal Engagement Teams is crucial. Remember, tribal honor codes mandate adherence to treaties and contracts, particularly between warriors who have fought side-by-side and risked their lives together.

A vast majority of the tribes just want to be left alone. Years and years of broken promises have severely damaged our ability to deal with the tribes. The Tribal Engagement Teams would show a commitment to the tribes and the tribal leadership that we will be unable to replicate in any other way. Putting US soldiers (TETs) on the ground with the tribes will say more about our commitment than anything else we can do. It will be a great "honor" and show them trust and respect by truly joining forces with them.

Bottom Line:

The GIRoA (Government of the Islamic Republic of Afghanistan) must find a way to incorporate the historical tribal structures into the national political system. It will not look like anything we can envision at this point, and may vary from province to province or even from tribe to tribe. But it can be done. Tribal Engagement Teams can help facilitate this.

7

TRIBES AND THE "ENEMY"

While most of the Taliban are from Pashtun tribes, the tribes themselves are not the enemy. The Taliban, al-Qaeda, HIG (Hezb-e Islami), Haqqani and other insurgent networks are the tribes' enemy—our enemy.

How Tribesmen Become Taliban

The Taliban find many willing recruits among disaffected tribesmen. The Taliban offer fame, glory and the chance to live exciting, meaningful lives. Many recruits see the Taliban as their only way to survive: Kill as a Taliban or be killed by the Taliban.

"By 2006, village jihadists accounted for fifteen to twenty-five percent of the Taliban's active fighting strength at any given time." (Giustozzi 2008, 43)

Our Tribal Engagement Teams (TETs) can get inside this disaffection/recruitment cycle and show the tribes that our teams (and by extension, the Coalition Forces and the Afghan central government) are there to help them. If we give them a better alternative—show them that we are their friends and are committed for the long haul—they will not only not attack us, but will be more willing to share intelligence and even come back home and fight for their tribe.

The Taliban Have Been Targeting the Tribes for Years

Taliban assassination teams have killed more than 120 tribal leaders in the past two years alone, and through intimidation driven many more away from their home districts. The practice of delivering "night letters"—written death threats—on tribal leaders' doorsteps is extremely effective. It's gangland, Afghan style. But the tribes are not all taking this passively; many are arming and organizing on their own, without US help.

The use of lashkars (Arbakai) is spreading, and we need to be there in the right way to join them as allies, not as intruders. "There is going to be a civil war. These lashkars are spreading," says Asfandyar Wali Khan, leader of the Awami National Party, which controls the provincial government in the NWFP.

"It will be the people versus the Taliban." (Wilkinson 2008)

The tribes are forming their own anti-Taliban fighting units, the Arbakai. Their main mission is to protect tribal homelands from any perceived threat (be that US forces, Afghan Army units, Afghan Police units, predatory warlords, al-Qaeda and the Taliban). With our assistance they will grow stronger and be far more effective—and be our allies. Don't we want to understand their motivations and influence them?

Engaging the tribes and understanding tribalism at its core is the surest and "lightest-footprint" opportunity we have to protect the tribes—the cultural and political foundation of Afghanistan—where they live, one tribe at a time. Doesn't it make sense to join forces with as many of them as we can, while at the same time gaining valuable intelligence on our enemies? This is a fundamental step in establishing the basis for order and security in this region.

"Pakistan has already armed some of the tribes in areas where the Taliban is attempting to move in. Some of these lashkars have as many as 14,000 members in the FATA (Federally Administrated

Tribal Areas) of Pakistan." (DeYoung 2008)

Many recruits see the Taliban as their only way to survive: Kill as a Taliban or be killed by the Taliban.

One tribal leader was recently quoted as saying, "I don't need tanks. I don't need planes. I don't even need a single bullet. I will use sticks and I will use the guns my people have to defend themselves." (Sappenfield 2008) Is that clear enough?

The enemy thinks he can wait us out. However, we can turn time into an ally if we engage and partner with the tribes and, most importantly, demonstrate our commitment to them.

Tribalism versus Talibanism

My team and I clearly proved it can be done. Malik Noor Afzhal and his people loved us. They enjoyed our stories and our culture. We were able to disprove many of their preconceived notions about "us" (outsiders, Americans, infidels or whatever).

When we left there, I promise you that the tribe in Mangwel thought very highly of Americans and what we represented, how we acted, and how we treated them. This is not just of tactical importance to understand, but strategic importance as well.

The enemy thinks he can wait us out. However, we can turn time into an ally if we engage and partner with the tribes and, most importantly, demonstrate our commitment to them. Once they believe that we share the same objectives and are not leaving, they will support us and fight alongside us.

"The Taliban is exploiting our major strategic…and tactical weakness: an inability to connect with the population (the tribes). Officials working in Pakistan and Afghanistan support this view, claiming that the youth 'oppose the current tribal system because they know it is not harnessing its potential.'" (Giustozzi 2008, 39)

My Tribal Engagement Strategy can beat the Taliban at its own game. "In its simplicity and effectiveness, the insurgents' reliance on small teams to infiltrate villages and weed out pro-Kabul elements was to prove one of the strongest aspects of the Taliban strategy. It pitted Taliban strength (abundance of commitment, ideologically indoctrinated young fighters able to achieve basic tasks even without supervision from field commanders) against government/ Coalition Forces weaknesses (shortage of manpower, little or no presence in the villages, inability to patrol extensively away from the main roads, and a lack of effective intelligence networks in most areas)." (Giustozzi 2008, 102)

We must help the tribes protect themselves by fighting alongside them. Will we make mistakes? Yes. But the risk is well worth the gain.

Bottom Line:

For the Afghan people, the real war is one of Tribalism vs. Talibanism. If we do not move now to support the tribes in this fight for their lives, it will produce a number of consequences, all of them bad: Taliban operations will expand over larger areas, killing more tribesmen and sweeping in more recruits as they go.

The one system in Afghanistan that has been reliable for centuries will continue to crumble, resulting in more disaffected tribal members drifting into terrorism and Islamic fundamentalism. Thus we will give up on the most critical element of Afghan society that can ultimately defeat the Taliban—the tribes. We simply cannot let this happen.

My Tribal Engagement Strategy can beat the Taliban at its own game.

8

HOW TO ENGAGE THE TRIBES

Rapport building and cross-cultural competency is the key.

If an important part of our strategy is to build working ground-level alliances with the tribes, how do we make this happen? My ODA 316 and I created a model for successful tribal engagement and all that it requires. The relationships I developed in Iraq and Afghanistan not only worked while we were there, they have stood the test of time and continue to this day. This chapter is all about how our model can be adapted successfully to similar situations anywhere.

First, let's look at an earlier example of successful tribal engagement. One of the main areas under contention today is in Southeast Afghanistan near Khas Khonar and the Pesch Valley areas. This is exactly where Sitting Bull's village of Mangwel is located. This same area was one of the British Empire's most challenging territories. How did they deal with it?

"From the 1890s to 1947, British control relied heavily on a small number of highly trained British officers. These frontier officers were highly educated, committed, conscientious, and hard working. Many had studied law and the history of the area and spoke some of the local languages. They had a deep sense of duty and a strong national identity. All required a depth of administrative competence and judgment to successfully wield the extensive powers at their disposal. They contributed significantly to the province's security and stability. These men were particularly valuable in navigating the intricacies of tribal politics." (Roe 2005, 20)

The key to a successful tribal engagement strategy is the ability to identify men (Tribal Engagement Team members) who have a special gift for cross-cultural competency and building rapport—that is, they must become educated in the ways of the tribes and build strong relationships with them based on mutual trust and objectives.

These men must like to fight and spend countless months, even years living in harsh circumstances. They will have to fully comprehend tribal concepts of honor, loyalty and revenge—the Pashtunwali code. Initially, they will have very little physical security other than the AK-47 they carry, their planning skills and the tribal fighters they live with.

Tribal Engagement Team (TET) Challenges

The situation at each tribe will be complex and will vary. Each will present its unique spider web of loyalties and subtle agendas that a Tribal Engagement Team must deal with smartly—and brutally when necessary. At the same time these men must be alert to detect and mediate local rivalries, sometimes within the tribe they are advising. They will have to be subjective on one issue and objective with another.

Five main problems we face in Afghanistan are:

The IED threat, the civilian casualties caused by air strikes, the inability of US forces to protect locals in rural areas, the immediate need for more Afghan and US troops, and the fact that we are losing the tactical and strategic information campaign there.

This tribal engagement plan addresses all five problems head on.

First, the IED threat will decrease to near zero because there will be little need to move troops around. The TETs will live in the village with the tribe. There will be no need to travel the dangerous roads between the firebases and the population.

Second, the TETs will be living with the tribe in its village, so calling in air strikes on your own village is not an option, unless the decision is made by the tribal leader in extreme circumstances. The tribal leader will be the final authority to make the call for air support, thus avoiding civilian casualties in his tribal domain.

Third, TETs living inside the village, not in some distant firebase, will increase the security of the village. The enemy will have to be much more aggressive to penetrate the tribal area, and that will dramatically increase the chances that we (the TET and Arbakai) will be able to kill them.

Fourth, the TETs will decrease the need for both US and Afghan government forces by training and advising a Tribal Security Force (TSF) or Arbakai. The Arbakai could be trained, equipped and organized as a modular, loose-knit unit. Eventually each TSF could be integrated into a kind of confederation—with district, regional and national units—to fight against any greater threat. Attack one tribe and you attack us all. This will take years to accomplish, but it will have tremendous enduring benefits for all concerned.

Fifth, the TETs must develop their own Information Operations and provide ground reports to all news media—the story has to be told. International media coverage of Muslim countries is extremely important. Seventy to eighty percent of the Afghan population cannot read, so videos and the spoken word in Pashto will be essential. This strategy will not work without a major Information Operations (IO) campaign.

Tactical Tribal Engagement

Tactical Tribal Engagement (TTE) is one possible solution in certain areas for the current problems facing the United States military in Afghanistan. This tactical strategy has far-reaching effects that will impact the operational and strategic nature of the war not only in Afghanistan, but across the border region of eastern Afghanistan and the ungoverned areas of the FATA (Federally Administered Tribal Areas) in Pakistan, specifically the northern FATA areas.

Essential TTE Tasks:

1. Establish and maintain rapport with the chosen tribe in the area. Advise and assist its leaders in all matters.

2. Provide real security for the village. Not presence patrols, but 24/7 on-site security. A permanent presence that the tribes can rely on. "Advise, assist, train, equip and lead" a TSF, an Arbakai.

3. Facilitate tactical civic action programs. Integration with the local Provincial Reconstruction Teams (PRTs) is crucial, along with the ability to use funds that units have at their disposal for "quick" money to help tribes who are facilitating the success of CF and the Afghan government. The TETs would also address basic healthcare and infrastructure services (water, electricity and irrigation), construction and repair of schools and clinics, both to improve

the life of the tribe and employ its individual members for pay. These programs should be worked through the local/district/provincial/national governments when possible and be integrated into the US battle space owner's overall plan.

4. Employ an aggressive tactical PSYOP plan that ties into the overall strategic IO campaign in the area. Tribes also can heavily counter the Taliban propaganda. This is a critical aspect of the success of the TTE strategy. The world has to see the Afghan tribes and US soldiers working, living, laughing, fighting and dying together.

5. Report "Ground Truth" continuously. This activity would tie the tribe in with all levels of the government system. It would also be the process by which the tribe's concerns are relayed directly to

the CF military apparatus. Such ongoing accounting would serve as a check and balance, reporting what is actually happening on the ground as opposed to what the GIRoA (Government of the Islamic Republic of Afghanistan) may say is happening. "Ground Truth" provides feedback to headquarters level units (battle space owners) in charge of the area ANA and ANP.

"I want the entire plan to be so effective that the Taliban feel threatened by our very presence, without us even firing a shot."

TET solutions should always be answers to local problems, yet always with an eye to integration with regional and national government representatives. It will also be imperative for TETs to watch for scenarios where local/district/provincial/national government forces can be successful. In other words, cooperate and help set the government up for success.

In return, the TSFs and tribal members would provide security, intelligence and early warning of insurgent attacks to the TETs, who would then pass this on to higher commands.

Mission Statement of a TET Leader:

I will train myself, my Tribal Engagement Team and my tribal counterpart for the tactical fight every single day.

I will establish strong, meaningful relationships with the tribal leaders.

My goal is to establish a relationship with my tribal counterpart, for my team to establish a strong relationship with the tribe; to establish focused security for the tribe and the locals in the area; to plan, develop and then implement a well-conceived IO, PSYOP and CA plan.

I want to make it so the Taliban and al-Qaeda have no choice but to come and meet us on our terms.

I want the entire plan to be so effective that the Taliban feel threatened by our very presence, without us even firing a shot.

A Key Requirement is to Tie the Tribe and the TET into the Following Areas:

- The local ANA and ANP.

- Provincial Reconstruction Teams (PRTs).

- National level Information Operations facilitators to include all major news agencies and publications.

- The local US forces (battle space owners).

- The ODA in the area.

- Higher echelon PSYOP units.

- Higher echelon CA units.

- Access to air assets for re-supply and CAS.

- NGOs

- Report "Ground Truth" to higher commands. Be the conduit of information and requests from the GIRoA and higher to and from the tribes. Report "Ground Truth" as well as the tribes' perceptions and expectations to the GIRoA and higher.

ONE TRIBE AT A TIME

The Key Tasks in Relation to the Tribal Leadership Will Be:

- Listen

- Understand

- Learn

- Influence

"Influence without Authority"

I could re-insert a Tribal Engagement Team in Mangwel tomorrow. However, in other areas it would take more time to perform a proper operational preparation of the battlefield (OPB) and build enough rapport to begin. There are many "acceptable" areas available. Acceptable does not mean no risk. This is not a strategy for the risk-averse. However, with the work we've done already, my TET would be safer in Mangwel than anywhere in Afghanistan.

Given the time and resources, I would go anywhere in the country and do this. It would take one month to prepare the TET for insertion into the area of operations (AO): I would need two weeks to do an analysis of the area (Area Study) and another two weeks to train my TET on the tactical tasks necessary to conduct the mission. The TET's goal is to achieve "influence without authority." The most reliable and lasting influence happens by acting as partners, not distant superiors or strangers.

The TSFs (Arbakai) will be a much more credible force than the local police (ANP) for many reasons. They will also give the villages and tribes what they need most: an accepted, professional force that can offer the tribe protection from the Taliban.

The relationships the TETs build with their tribes will have long-lasting effects, free of influence or interference by local/district/provincial/national politics. The TET/TSF alliance will be able to govern and secure the tribe's area until the tribe is confident that the local police and army can help protect them. Even then the tribes will be able to maintain their autonomy.

Afghan tribes do not give up their autonomy to anyone. Many, many tribal militias fought against the presence of the Taliban long before 9/11.

The TET will also need to monitor closely the relationship the tribe has with other tribes in the area, and how they are interacting. Of course, the goal is to incorporate as many other tribes as possible into the TTE strategy and give each tribe a TET. That is the major goal of the expansion phase of the operation.

Why chase the enemy? Make him come to us. And when I say "us" I mean a group of people who have the same goals: the TET and the tribe.

Influence without authority – Sitting Bulll and I
enjoyed each other's company. Our camaraderie set
the tone for out team's relationship with the rest of
the tribe. We laughed and spoke of many things that
most US forces are taught as being taboo.

Make no mistake, there is a lot more
fighting and killing to do. We should do
it on our terms, side by side with Afghans
with as many advantages as we can have.
The TTE strategy will give us that.

This plan requires a small group of men who
can comprehend the extensive networks,
influences and idiosyncrasies of the mission

and the environment. We're talking about "street smarts"—the instinct to grasp and account for all second, third and fourth order effects of decisions at all levels.

This is warfare at the Ph.D. level. It is constantly changing and requires continual assessment. Only a few dedicated men can execute this plan properly.

It will become a very personal fight. Once we commit to the tribe, the Pashtunwali code comes into effect for the US team as well. In the end it will be the TET's ability to build a true bond with the tribe that is backed up by warrior ethos: the ability and desire to fight and die alongside them when necessary.

Start Small, Think Big

This strategy can be tested on a pilot basis. It doesn't have to cost a lot of money. Tactical Tribal Engagement can be tried out on a small-scale (one or two tribes in a given area) to determine how productive it will be for the long term. It will take at least six months to a year to see any tangible results. Once it is demonstrated that this course of action will work, more resources can be put into it for the long-term (three to five years). I think everyone agrees that Afghanistan will not be won overnight. This strategy requires an investment of time, but not major manpower or resources.

Sitting Bulll, Dr. Akhbar and I enjoyed many late-night conversations in the midst of our tribal friends.

We helped the tribe with village projects whenever we could. ODA 316 built this well for Dr. Akhbar.

Even if the TTE strategy does not work on a large scale, wouldn't ten or twenty successes impact the overall COIN fight in Afghanistan? I believe the answer is yes. As a matter of fact, success in Mangwel is almost a guarantee if I can get there before Malik Noor Afzhal passes away. He is eighty-six years old and time is ticking.

Now, as always, the enemy has a vote as well. As the TETs and TSFs become more of a threat, the more the Taliban will increase the time, resources, capacity and will to destroy or at least disrupt their operation. This will increase the overall threat and in turn the violence directed at both the TET and the tribe.

The Risks of Tactical Tribal Engagement

Each TET tribe will become a target and will take casualties. The US teams themselves will be targeted. There will be fighting. But the fighting will be US soldiers alongside tribesmen against a common enemy. Isn't that what we want?

There will also be "push-back" from assorted Afghan officials, powerbrokers, warlords, criminals, and some minority races in Afghanistan, as we would be arming and training a majority of Pashtun tribes.

How do we Deal with Competing Tribes?

One of the keys here is to ensure that we tie what we are doing at the tactical level to regional and national representatives. Not coordinating our goals and operations with Afghanistan's national political/military elements only promotes a confusing and contentious relationship between the various government entities and the tribal system.

> *Each TET tribe will become a target and will take casualties. The US teams themselves will be targeted. There will be fighting. But the fighting will be US soldiers alongside tribesmen against a common enemy. Isn't that what we want?*

From top to ground level, we ideally must be on the "same page" and move forward as one united force.

My last thought on the long-term effect of this strategy is that of the Chinese bamboo tree...

When a Chinese bamboo tree is planted, the grower must water and nurture it. The first year, it does not grow more than one inch above the ground. During the second year, after more watering and fertilizing, the tree does not grow any more than it did during year one. The bamboo tree is still no more than one inch high after four years. Nothing tangible can be seen by any outsider.

But, in the fifth year, the tree can grow more than eighty feet. Of course, the first four years the tree was growing its roots, deep into the ground. It is the roots that enable the tree to create an explosion of growth in year five.

Bottom Line: A TET strategy will have to be given the time and patience to do its work. But as our teams continue to establish themselves, one tribe at a time, their influence will reach a tipping point and become a far-reaching strategic influence.

The Original Six. This is not a good quality photograph—taken in near dark with a marginal camera—but it may be the only picture I have of the original six members of ODA 316. Yes, there were only six of us during our first three months of fighting in Mangwel.

Clockwise from me sitting down in front: SFC Mark Read above my right shoulder, then SFC Chuck Burroughs, SSG Dan McKone, SSG Tony Siriwardene, SSG Scott Gross on Tony's left, and finally that is Khalid, my outstanding interpreter, sitting below Scott.

I have always loved this picture as it was these six men who started what would become a great fighting unit that found Sitting Bull and a new way to fight the Taliban in Afghanistan.

TRIBAL ENGAGEMENT TEAM TIMELINE

The first timeline noted below moves the TET into an area that supports US presence or a TET member who already has strong ties in the area (like Mangwel). I call this a *permissive scenario.*

The second scenario is one where the tribal members are neutral to US support or there is no prior relationship with TET members entering the area. In this case, the timeline would be pushed out from three to nine additional months. This situation would be a *semi-permissive scenario.*

The permissive and semi-permissive scenario is in relation to the tribe, not the environment itself. Although the tribe may be permissive (receptive) to the TET, the overall environment may be semi-permissive or even non-permissive. The fact may be that a particular tribe may want the TET, yet be surrounded by tribes that may not. Or the Taliban may have support in an area where the tribes support the TET.

By far the most important daily task is building rapport. This is our security. This is what will allow the TET to accomplish "influence without authority."

Permissive Environment Phases with Timeline:

The Taliban will know immediately when a tribe receives some sort of US team and that the team is living inside the village with a tribe.

1. **Preparation Phase (1-2 months):** The TET begins its Operational Preparation of the Battlefield (OPB) development.

Information gathering (area study), intelligence collection and analysis, intensive language training, logistics planning, detailed logistics request.

Tactical train-up with TET members.

2. **Infiltration, Rapport and Organization Phase (1 month):** The TET assesses and develops relationships in the tribe and begins training the TSF (Arbakai).

Infiltration. The TET would move into the closest firebase (FB) to a selected tribal area and begin its tactical Intelligence Preparation of the Battlefield and continue its training.

Initial Contact. This would vary based on the enemy threat and the history of the area. In Mangwel my team and I could show up completely unannounced and it would work. In other areas the TET may have to request a meeting with the tribal leader or possibly even send a local

ANA/ANP unit to the village to request that the head malik come to the firebase to talk.

Determine with the tribal leaders how many TSF (Arbakai) members they want, how many they need and what the TET can realistically support and train.

3. **Assessment and Build-up Phase (6 to 8 months):** The TET begins to build a true relationship with the tribe by this time and can make a much better assessment of the ways and means of the tribe. Focus is on the training program for the TSF and security posture of the TET. This period will be the most dangerous for the TET as it will become apparent that the tribe is receiving outside support and becoming a threat to any enemy in the area. The threat to the tribe and the TET will increase in direct proportion to the success of the TET's integration with the tribe.

4. **Expansion and Sustainment Phase (continuous, open-ended time frame):** During this phase the biggest strides will be made by integrating the tribe into the local/district/regional and national government because they will be secure and, most importantly, they will feel respected and honored because the US has shown a clear commitment to them.

   How to choose the right tribes to partner with? One good way is using "will" and "capacity" as benchmarks for initial screening. Some tribes have both the will and capacity to fight the Taliban. Other tribes have the will but not the capacity. Other tribes have the capacity and not the will.

What about the Tajiks, the Hazaras, and the Uzbeks?

Do we support some of those tribes as well? I believe we should.

There is also the issue of key terrain located in a specific tribal area, and even areas the Taliban may need for various reasons (opium, supply and infiltration routes, etc.). The decision to support which tribe(s) would be an Afghan one. We (the US) also would need to put our own analysts and criteria to it to ensure that the right decisions were being made.

The method of performance (MOP) and the method of evaluation (MOE) criteria actually will not be that difficult to determine for the TET. However, as the RAND study points out, "Effective analysis capability is a critical component of any capability. Counterinsurgency operations require the development of an analytical methodology to measure the insurgency's impact on the local population—especially the impact of the security condition. Several factors can make it difficult to measure the effectiveness of counterinsurgency operations: Progress cannot be measured by the advance of militaries across a map as in conventional warfare; focusing only on guerrilla fighters misses the broader support network; a complicated array of political, economic, social, and military factors can fuel the insurgency; and there are rarely ideal predefined qualitative or quantitative target metrics." (Jones 2008, 122)

Every Day the Tribal Engagement Team Will Focus on Security and Quality of Life Issues

A major concern is initial security. This must be built from the inside out. Our influence comes not just from providing security or enabling the tribe to provide it themselves. It is the fact that we are there. We are living with the tribe, sharing their dangers and hardships. This does not require a massive footprint. A very small team can accomplish miracles. I have seen it and I have done it.

After a relationship has been built with the tribes, we will be able to gather relevant and actionable intelligence on the Taliban, HIG, Haqqani and al-Qaeda networks in Afghanistan and Pakistan. The tribe and the Tribal Security Force and specially trained tribesmen who live among the population are in a position to gather information and intelligence. Make no mistake about it, these tribesmen have the ability to collect the type of intelligence we need to be successful.

The TETs need the latitude to dress, speak and act in the ways that will maximize their acceptance by the tribes. This may mean wearing local garb, growing beards, and interacting with the tribe on a personal level. They must be able to "go native." Go to the tribe's elementary school daily. Learn Pashto from them. Learn about being a Muslim. Learn about Islam. Learn about the tribe. Ideally, TETs must not only live with the tribe, but steadily integrate themselves into tribal life and customs (as much as the tribe allows). My experience in Mangwel would not be believed by most who did not see it firsthand.

Targeting Taliban and al-Qaeda will be a secondary, but at times needed, task.

The Tribal Security Force (Arbakai) Would Have Three Primary Elements:

1. A security force responsible for the physical safety of the village/tribe members.

2. An intelligence collection element (kishakee).

3. An offensive action and reconnaissance element. This element could integrate itself with ANA or CF elements with the help of the TETs.

The initial priority would be to quickly mobilize the TSFs. They can become an effective force in a short period of time, possibly in ninety days.

Paying the TSF will automatically improve the financial situation of the village and create a stronger bond with the tribesmen who live there.

Task Organization

The following is a "shopping list" of what I, or any TET leader, would need on Day One:

- 3/6/12 US personnel based on environment

- 2 interpreters

- 2 SAT phones

- 2 SATCOM radio (piggyback freq)

- 2 PRC-119s

- 2 ATVs

- 2 Pick-up trucks

- 3 Generators

- 2 Computers with a biometrics kit

Initial infill logistics package for the tribe:

- 100 AK-47s

- 30,000 to 50,000 rounds of ammunition

- Assorted medical supplies

- A "Gift of Honor" for the tribal chief

One must have a true love and respect for the Afghan people (the tribes) and be willing to give a better part of his life for this strategy to work. Not everyone will be able to do this nor should they. But for those warriors who are qualified and feel the calling, it will be the adventure of a lifetime.

Someday you too could fly an American flag outside your firebase, as we did at ours here in Asadabad.

9

CLOSING THOUGHTS

"Many so-called failed states are really failed tribes."

-David Ronfeldt, "Tribes—
The First and Forever Form"

We have to study and understand the tribes. Become their true friends and let them see us in all of our strengths and faults as well.

Work with Tribalism, Not Against It

"In the absence of state institutions, how can a typical civil society's service requirements be provided or administered in an efficient manner? One way is to use traditional groups such as tribes who have experience in performing local governance roles and functions." (Taylor 2005, 9)

In the words of Haji Mohammed Zalmay, one of the better district governors in Konar Province, "The key to success is getting tribes to come to shuras and keeping them united."

Remember, in most cases the Taliban is not present in areas where the tribes do not want them to be.

Whether the US "wins" or "loses" in Afghanistan, the tribes will still be there. As David Ronfeldt says in "Tribes—The First and Forever Form," "The tribe will never lose its significance or its attractiveness; it is not going away in the centuries ahead." Therefore, we must learn to understand the tribe's significance *now*.

There will be no large-scale "awakening" of the tribes in Afghanistan, as there was in al-Anbar Province in Iraq. It will be a much lower and more difficult process.

Nine Differences between Iraq and Afghanistan

In an excellent paper by Carter Malkasian and Jerry Meyerle entitled, "How is Afghanistan different from al-Anbar?" the authors list nine differences and four implications of those differences:

1. Sectarianism in Iraq versus government misrule in Afghanistan

2. The strength of Arab tribes in al-Anbar versus Pashtun tribes in Afghanistan

3. Afghanistan's unique history of warlordism

4. The major rift in the al-Anbar insurgency versus the minor rifts in the Afghan insurgency

5. Arab tribal customs in Iraq versus the Pashtun tribal code (Pashtunwali) in Afghanistan

6. The urban al-Anbar insurgency versus the rural Afghan insurgency

7. The IED and suicide attacks of the Anbar insurgents versus the small-unit tactics of the Afghan insurgents [Note: this point is not as valid in 2009 as it was in 2007.]

8. Fuel smuggling in al-Anbar versus the poppy trade in Afghanistan

9. The cross-border sanctuaries surrounding al-Anbar versus Pakistan's tribal areas

We must learn to understand the tribe's significance now.

Four Implications of These Differences

1. Government misrule and warlordism define the problem in Afghanistan. Without reducing the abusive behavior of the government and their warlord clients, it is hard to see how security measures will have a long-lasting effect.

2. Together, the large sanctuary in Pakistan's tribal area and the poppy trade make the insurgency resilient. They may have the wherewithal to go round after round, fighting season after fighting season.

3. The fragmented nature of the tribal system, the absence of a major rift between tribes and the insurgents, and the feuding of Pashtunwali demand patience and forethought in the planning and execution of tribal engagement efforts. Small scale community successes are more likely than large-scale province-wide successes.

4. Pashtunwali, a rural environment, and the tactical skills of the insurgency call for a re-thinking of the tactics of counterinsurgency. Some tactics, most notably cordon and searches, air strikes, and population control measures may need to be restrained. Because of Pashtunwali, their costs may exceed their benefits.

"It's the Tribes, Stupid"

Steven Pressfield's videos/writings on tribalism are the most useful resources I have found on understanding tribalism. The author of *Gates of Fire* and *The Afghan Campaign* has a blog called "It's the Tribes, Stupid," which provides the historical and conceptual context for a tribal engagement strategy in Afghanistan.

See it at http://blog.stevenpressfield.com.

What Scares Me Most

On a personal note, my gravest concern is that a Tribal Engagement Strategy in some form will indeed be adopted and implemented, but that the US may eventually again abandon Afghanistan— and the tribes to whom we have promised long-term support will be left to be massacred by a vengeful Taliban.

> *I will get on a helicopter tonight, armed with an AK-47 and three hundred rounds of ammunition, and put my life on the line and my strategy to the test. Will you do the same?*

This is by far the worst outcome we could have.

It is immoral and unethical to ask a tribe to help us and promise them support and then leave them to defend themselves on their own. If our forces do withdraw from Afghanistan, we should decide now to arm

ONE TRIBE AT A TIME

the tribes who support us with enough
weapons and ammunition to survive after
we leave.

A Commitment to the Tribes and People of Afghanistan

I emphasized at the beginning of this
paper that I am neither a strategist nor
an academic. I know there will be many
criticisms that span all levels of war, from
military personnel to pundits.

But I also know this: I will get on a
helicopter tonight, armed with an AK-47
and three hundred rounds of ammunition
and put my life on the line and my strategy
to the test. Will you do the same?

Bottom Line:

There may be dozens of reasons not to adopt
this strategy. But there is only one reason to
do so—we have to. Nothing else will work.

ACKNOWLEDGMENTS

First and foremost I want to thank the great warriors of ODA 316. It seems like so long ago. No one will ever believe how much we did with so little in those early days in the Konar. We have all continued to fight and have taken it to the enemy at every opportunity. Leading you was the greatest honor of my life.

Initial members of ODA 316 (by rank):

Ron Bryant

Al Lapene

Chuck Burroughs

Mark Read

Tony Siriwardene

Scott Gross

Dan McKone

James Tierney

Travis Weitzel

Luke Murray

Brent Watson

Dave Casson

Second, my good friend Steve Pressfield. Only he knows what his words have meant to me. I would not have done this without him. He is a great author and historian. He is a better friend.

Third, my wife. She has put up with all the long deployments and all the "baggage" that comes with that. And thanks for all the hours you let me spend in front of the computer just before my upcoming deployment in Iraq.

Fourth, my dad. "The best team always wins…"

Lastly, my second "father," friend, fellow warrior and great leader, Malik Noor Afzhal, "Sitting Bull." It was my greatest wish in all the world that I would get to see him with my own eyes again and say, "Sitting Bull, I told you I would come back. I told you I would return." I could have died a happy man had that happened.

REFERENCES

Sappenfield, Mark. 2008. "To Fight Taliban, US Eyes Afghan Tribes." *The Christian Science Monitor*, October 16. http://www.csmonitor.com/World/Asia-South-Central/2008/1016/p01s04-wosc.html

Cowell, Alan. 2009 "US General Says Allies 'Not Winning' Afghan War." *New York Times*, March 9. http://www.nytimes.com/2009/03/10/world/asia/10afghan.html?_r=0

Pressfield, Steven. "It's the Tribes, Stupid." http://www.stevenpressfield.com/vblog/

Ronfeldt, David. 2006. "Tribes—The First and Forever Form." *RAND Corporation*, December: 5, 7, 29, 35, 39, 59, 65, 68, 72, 73, 76. http://www.rand.org/content/dam/

rand/pubs/working_papers/2007/RAND_
WR433.pdf

McCallister, William. 2008. "Operations in
Pakistan's Tribal Areas," *Small Wars Journal*,
January 30: 4, 7. http://smallwarsjournal.
com/blog/operations-in-pakistans-tribal-
areas.

Malkasian, Carter, and Meyerle, Jerry.
2009. "How is Afghanistan Different from
Al Anbar?" *CNA Analysis and Solutions*
(February): 5-7, 11. http://www.dtic.mil/
dtic/tr/fulltext/u2/a498368.pdf

Yusufzai, Rahimullah. "Help the Pashtuns."
Foreign Policy Magazine. A daily newspaper
in Peshawar.

Jones, Seth G. 2008 "Counterinsurgency
in Afghanistan." *RAND Counterinsurgency
Study* 4: xiii, xi, 7, 10, 122.

Moreau, Ron, and Yousafzai, Sami. 2009. "Obama's Vietnam," *Newsweek* (February): 32-33.

Kilcullen, David. 2008. "It's still winnable, but only just," *Interesting Times* (November 14).

Kelly, Justin. 2009. "How to Win Afghanistan," *Quadrant* (April 1): 5. http://www.quadrant.org.au/magazine/issue/2009/4/how-to-win-in-Afghanistan

Rosenau, William. 2008. "Low-Cost Trigger-Pullers," *RAND National Security Research Division* (October): p.22

Giustozzi, Antonio. 2008. *Koran, Kalashnikov, and Laptop.* New York: Columbia University Press.

Tariq, Mohammad Osman. 2008. "Tribal Security System (Arbakai) in Southeast Afghanistan," Crisis States Research Centre (December): 10.

Wilkinson, Marwat. 2008. "Tribal Chief Takes on Taliban with His Own Army," *London Daily Telegraph* (September 23): 14.

DeYoung. 2008. "Pakistan Will Give Arms to Tribal Militias," *Washington Post* (October 23): 1.

Roe, Major Andrew M. British Army. 2005. "To Create a Stable Afghanistan: Provincial Reconstruction Teams, Good Governance, and a Splash of History," *Military Review* (November-December): 20.

2009. "Obama Keeps Karzai at Arm's Length," *The Washington Post* (May 6).

Taylor, Richard L. 2005. "Tribal Alliances: Ways, Means, and Ends to Successful Strategy," Strategic Studies Institute (August): 9.

Made in the USA
Middletown, DE
27 August 2015